The Library at Warwick School
Please return or renew on or before the last date
below

3/19

OUR WORLD IN CRISIS

CIVIL WAR & GENOCIDE

IZZI HOWELL

FRANKLIN WATTS
LONDON•SYDNEY

Franklin Watts
First published in Great Britain in 2018 by The Watts Publishing Group
Copyright © The Watts Publishing Group, 2018

Produced for Franklin Watts by
White-Thomson Publishing Ltd
www.wtpub.co.uk

ISBN: 978 1 4451 6371 0

Credits
Series Editor: Izzi Howell
Series Designer: Dan Prescott, Couper Street Type Co.
Series Consultant: Philip Parker

The publisher would like to thank the following for permission to reproduce their
pictures: Alamy: ITAR-TASS Photo Agency *cover*, Barry Iverson 11, richard harvey 13,
REUTERS 18 and 43, Wamodo 19, Stocktrek Images, Inc. 28, Andrew Aitchison 31,
Prisma by Dukas Presseagentur GmbH 42, Richard Smith 45; Getty: Christian
Marquardt 37; Shutterstock: Christiaan Triebert *title page* and 9, Nathan Holland 4,
Everett Historical 7, Andreas R. 14, Asianet-Pakistan 15, Northfoto 16 and 40, Adnan
Vejzovic 17 and 47, ART production 21, hikrcn 22, Orlok 2 and 23, Procyk Radek 25,
blurAZ 26, M. W. Hunt 35, Lenscap Photography 36, punghi 39, Gail Palethorpe 41,
Nelliapoyan 44; US Army (USA) Training Support Center/MARLENE THOMPSON,
CIV, FORT GORDON, USA 12.

All design elements from Shutterstock.

Every attempt has been made to clear
copyright. Should there be any
inadvertent omission please apply
to the publisher for rectification.

Printed in China

Franklin Watts
An imprint of
Hachette Children's Group
Part of The Watts Publishing Group
Carmelite House
50 Victoria Embankment
London EC4Y 0DZ

An Hachette UK Company
www.hachette.co.uk
www.franklinwatts.co.uk

CONTENTS

Modern

CIVIL WARS

Up until the beginning of the twentieth century, most wars were international. They were fought between different countries or states. For example, Great Britain, France, Russia and the USA fought against Germany and Austria-Hungary in the First World War (1914–1918).

However, since the end of the Second World War in 1945, most wars have been civil wars. Civil wars are fought between different groups of people within the same country or state.

The end of colonies

After the world wars, many countries gained independence from the European countries that had once colonised them. Some countries only gained independence by defeating their former colonial rulers in battle. Once the colonial rulers had been removed, the victorious rebels had to decide who would take control. New political groups formed and scrambled to gain power. This often led to civil wars in these countries.

In Angola, abandoned tanks and other remains of the civil war are still visible, even though the conflict ended in 2002.

CASE STUDY

The Angolan civil war

In 1975, one year after the end of Angola's war of independence from Portugal (1961-1974), civil war broke out between three former independence parties. Despite multiple attempts to get the three parties to reach a peace agreement, the war raged on for 27 years until 2002. Over 1.5 million people died in the conflict and 4 million people had to leave their homes.

New rulers

After decolonisation, new rulers often had a weak hold over their country. They hadn't had time to show that they could run the country well. Former colonies were often left with a poor economy and a weakened army. This made it easier for other competing groups from within the country to gain popularity and challenge the rule of the existing rulers, potentially starting a civil war in the process.

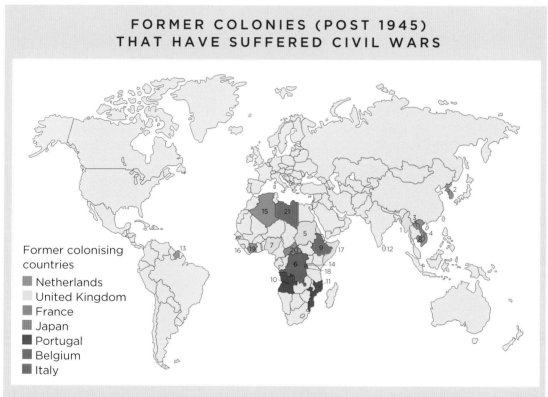

FORMER COLONIES (POST 1945) THAT HAVE SUFFERED CIVIL WARS

Former colonising countries

- Netherlands
- United Kingdom
- France
- Japan
- Portugal
- Belgium
- Italy

1) Myanmar 1948–present
2) Korea 1950–1953
3) Laos 1954–1975
4) Vietnam 1954–1976
5) Sudan 1955–1972 and 1983–2005
6) Democratic Republic of Congo 1960–1965 and 1997–2003
7) Nigeria 1967–1970
8) Cambodia 1970–1975
9) Ethiopia 1974–1991
10) Angola 1975–2002
11) Mozambique 1976–1992
12) Sri Lanka 1983–2009
13) Suriname 1986–1992
14) Rwanda 1990–1993
15) Algeria 1991–1999
16) Sierra Leone 1991–2002
17) Somalia 1991–present
18) Burundi 1994–2005
19) Ivory Coast 2002–2007
20) Central African Republic 2012–present
21) Libya 2014–present

Different societies

Many civil wars in the twentieth century were brought about by the clash of communism and capitalism. In a communist society, the government controls the production of all goods and wealth is, in theory, equally divided among citizens. In capitalist countries, individuals work and produce goods for their own personal profit. The life that you lead depends on the amount of money that you earn.

Capitalism vs Communism

After the Second World War, the USA and the Soviet Union were very powerful. The Soviet Union was communist, while the USA was capitalist. When communist or capitalist groups in other countries became involved in civil wars, the Soviet Union and the USA often stepped in to support the cause of communism or capitalism. The Soviet Union wanted to help communism spread across the world, while the USA was determined to stop it.

 **THE USA AND SOVIET UNION WERE INVOLVED IN THE FOLLOWING 'CIVIL WARS':**

VIETNAM (1954–1976)   **CONGO (1960–1965)**   **ETHIOPIA (1974–1991)**

The Cold War

These wars were officially called 'civil wars' because they took place between two groups in the same country. However, some people consider that these wars were really proxy wars – a way for the Soviet Union and the USA to fight each other, without declaring an official war. This struggle between the Soviet Union and the USA was known as the Cold War (approx. 1947–1991). During the Cold War, the two countries fought each other without actually attacking each other directly. No one wanted a real war between the Soviet Union and the USA, as both sides held deadly nuclear weapons.

CASE STUDY

The Korean War

After the Second World War, the Soviet Union ran the north of Korea while the USA controlled the south. Both parts of the country organised armies and in June 1950, the North Korean army invaded the south. The USA supported the south, while communist China sent troops to join the northern army. More than a million people died in the fighting, which ended three years later. After the war, the north and the south split into two separate countries. Today, South Korea has a successful capitalist economy, while North Korea is still ruled as a communist dictatorship in which thousands of people suffer from persecution and hunger.

The Cold War ends

From 1989 onwards, the Soviet Union started to split apart into individual countries, such as Russia, Ukraine and Latvia. The Cold War between the Soviet Union and the USA gradually came to an end, although there are still tensions between Russia and the USA today.

Thousands of refugees fled from North Korea to South Korea when the fighting started. Some returned to North Korea at the end of the war.

Money and power

Many civil wars are driven by greed for money and power. Today, these conflicts often happen in countries that are rich in natural resources, such as Liberia, which has many diamond mines. Corrupt leaders want to take control of a country so that they can get rich personally from selling its resources. They may do so through violence, starting a civil war between their troops and the country's army.

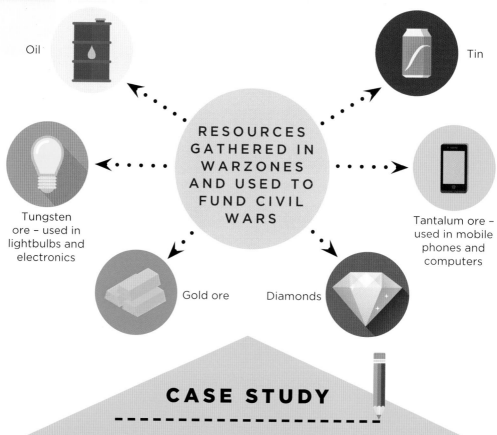

Oil

Tin

RESOURCES GATHERED IN WARZONES AND USED TO FUND CIVIL WARS

Tungsten ore – used in lightbulbs and electronics

Tantalum ore – used in mobile phones and computers

Gold ore   Diamonds

CASE STUDY

Liberian blood diamonds

Liberia, in West Africa, is rich in natural resources such as gold, rubber and diamonds. Charles Taylor became president of Liberia in 1997, after rebelling against the government in the first Liberian civil war (1989-1996). As president, he became wealthy through the sale of diamonds. He used this money to pay for weapons and ammunition. Such diamonds became known as blood diamonds – diamonds taken from warzones and used to fund wars. In 2001, sanctions were placed on the Liberian diamond trade to prevent the sale of blood diamonds. Now that Charles Taylor is in prison for war crimes, Liberia is trying to rebuild its diamond industry.

Ethnic conflicts

Civil wars can happen between different ethnic groups in the same country. In the civil war that split apart the former Republic of Yugoslavia, the fighting was divided on ethnic lines between Bosnian Muslims, Serbs, Croats and Albanians. There had been a long history of conflict between the Tutsi and Hutu ethnic groups in Rwanda before civil war broke out between them in 1990 (see page 31).

Separate states

Ethnic groups sometimes wish to split apart from a country and create their own state. Having a separate state would give them their own identity, make them feel safer and allow them to create their own rules. In the Sri Lankan civil war (1983–2009), the Tamil ethnic group fought the government to create their own independent state, after years of discrimination. However, they were unsuccessful, and the original government still rules today.

Corruption and rebellion

Some civil wars begin as peaceful protests against corrupt and authoritarian regimes, before becoming violent. Before the recent conflict in Syria, people wanted a more democratic society, so they started a rebellion against the restrictive government. In 2011, this turned into a civil war.

The Syrian city of Azaz lays in ruins after years of conflict, like many other cities in the country.

What can you do?

It can be upsetting to hear about people suffering in wars, but it's important to stay informed. Find out the latest news on civil wars around the world in newspapers, on social media apps such as Twitter or on websites, such as http://www.bbc.co.uk/newsround.

Before a civil war begins, there is usually a period of tension between the different sides. There may be a few violent incidents, threats or last-minute attempts to resolve the situation peacefully. Then, suddenly, something dramatic happens that changes the situation altogether and war is declared.

Coups

Many civil wars begin with a coup (pronunciation – coo). 'Coup' is a shortened version of 'coup d'état' – a French phrase that means 'hit of the state'. During a coup, a group makes a sudden, illegal attempt to take control of a country from the current rulers.

Coups are often led by a small group of military leaders or powerful politicians. These people have lots of power and can use it to gain control. If a coup fails, it can lead to civil war, as the ruling party tries to silence the other side and punish them for their betrayal.

For example, the Spanish civil war began in 1936, when the military tried and failed to take control from the government. Following the attempted coup, civil war broke out between the military, led by Francisco Franco, and the Spanish government. Franco was to rule Spain as a dictator until 1975.

Revolutions

In a revolution, ordinary people rise up against their government and try to change the politics of their country. This could be to improve the social or economic situation in a country or to get rid of a government or dictator. In some cases, such as in Libya in 2011, the existing government sent soldiers to attack revolutionary protesters. If members of the revolution decide to fight back, a civil war has begun.

CASE STUDY

The Arab Spring

The Arab Spring was a series of uprisings beginning in December 2010 against governments in northern African and Middle Eastern countries. They were mainly carried out by young people, who organised themselves and shared ideas on social media. The protesters wanted a more peaceful and democratic system of government. At first, the uprisings seemed to have a positive effect and led to changes in government in Tunisia, Egypt, Yemen, Libya and Syria. However, as time went on, the governments of these countries started to fight back against the protesters, leading to civil wars and violent conflicts.

Thousands of pro-democracy protesters took to the streets in Cairo, Egypt, in April 2011 to show their support for the Arab Spring uprisings.

New groups

The outbreak of war can give rebel groups an opportunity to gain power. In the Syrian civil war, a new extremist Islamist group called ISIS has joined the fighting. They are fighting against the government and the protestors who organised the Arab Spring uprising. ISIS is trying to gain new territory and force people to follow their extreme rules.

In most civil wars, one side is significantly smaller than the other. This is known as asymmetric warfare. However, having a larger fighting force does not guarantee victory in any war.

Different sides

Usually, a country's existing rulers or government have the national military on their side. They have access to a large number of trained soldiers, weapons and resources. The opposing side often has a smaller militia, made up of civilians or trained soldiers who aren't part of a country's army. They have less money to buy weapons and supplies.

Weapon technology

Trained soldiers in civil wars today have access to the latest weapons technology. They fight with highly accurate and deadly weapons, such as tanks and drones. If civilians join in with the fighting, they are armed with basic weapons, such as knives, machetes and homemade bombs. Some groups will send civilians to training camps to make them more effective soldiers.

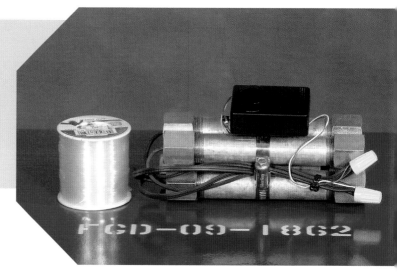

Pipe bombs are a common type of homemade bomb. Metal pipes are stuffed with explosive material and a fuse attached to a timer. This picture shows a fake pipe bomb used to train US soldiers.

International involvement

Other countries sometimes participate in civil wars. Although they are not officially involved, they can help a side become more powerful by supplying them with weapons. Some countries even fight on behalf of the side that they support. For example, Russia has been carrying out airstrikes to assist the Syrian government in their civil war, while the USA has carried out airstrikes against ISIS in Iraq. In this way, other countries can influence the outcome of a war.

Illegal weapons

Some armies have been accused of using illegal weapons during civil wars. All types of chemical weapon, such as tear gas and nerve gas, are banned around the world. However, there is very strong evidence that sarin gas has been used by the government in the Syrian civil war. People exposed to sarin gas experience confusion, paralysis and eventually death.

These soldiers from the Free Syrian Army (FSA) are opposing the Syrian government in the civil war. Turkey has supplied the FSA with troops and weapons, such as machine guns.

Quick and quiet

Smaller armies can use their size to their advantage. Although they have fewer soldiers, they can move around quickly and quietly. This makes it easy for them to carry out surprise attacks. This approach is sometimes known as guerrilla warfare. Typical guerrilla attacks include raids, sabotage and assassinations. In this way, a few people can do a huge amount of damage. However, they are at risk of becoming outnumbered, as this is where large armies are at an advantage.

This tour guide is showing the hidden entrance to a Viet Cong tunnel.

Terrorism

Acts of terrorism, such as suicide bombings, are often common in the build-up to, and during, civil wars. Groups that claim to be motivated by politics or religion carry out these acts to scare ordinary people or manipulate them into agreeing with their viewpoint. Terrorism is widely reported in the media and it has a great impact on many people.

Sometimes, a group will admit to having carried out a terrorist act. They want to show people that they are powerful and that it is dangerous to oppose them. On other occasions, a group will blame the act on their rivals. This is a type of propaganda – false information that a group gives out in order to damage and discredit rival groups. By blaming the terrorism on their enemies, they convince ordinary people that the rival organisation is a threat and, therefore, should be defeated.

Police inspect the scene of a suicide bombing in Pakistan. Many terrorist attacks in Pakistan are carried out by Tehrik-e Taleban Pakistan (TTP), an anti-government terrorist group.

Peacekeeping troops

The United Nations (UN) is an international organisation that protects human rights (see pages 26–29). If the UN believes that soldiers may start attacking civilians during a civil war, it may send peacekeeping troops to protect them. Peacekeeping troops do not support either side in a war. They come from other countries that belong to the UN. Some members of the UN have to supply a certain number of soldiers for this role.

Keeping the peace

Peacekeeping troops are trained to help both sides sort out their differences in a non-violent way. They encourage troops to call a ceasefire, where both sides stop fighting each other. They have a responsibility to protect civilians from human rights abuses during war, for example to stop civilians becoming the victims of genocide (the killing of a large number of people from an ethnic, religious, national or racial group).

Italian peacekeeping troops from the UN help to evacuate a woman from Sarajevo, during the conflict there following the break-up of Yugoslavia (1992–1996).

CASE STUDY

The Srebrenica massacre

UN peacekeeping troops are not always successful at protecting civilians. One of their greatest failures was not preventing the Srebrenica massacre during the civil war caused by the break-up of Yugoslavia. The UN had declared the town of Srebrenica a safe zone and so many civilians remained there. However, the UN had not provided enough troops to defend the civilians in Srebrenica from the Bosnian Serb army. In July 1995, the Bosnian Serb army marched on Srebrenica and murdered over 8,000 Muslim Bosnian men and boys.

This cemetery is the final resting place for some of the victims of the Srebrenica massacre. Their bodies were originally buried in mass graves, but after the war, their families recovered their remains and reburied them properly.

Charities

Many charities intervene in civil wars and conflicts. They provide aid and support for the civilians living in warzones. The International Red Cross and Red Crescent Movement sends doctors to give medical attention to injured civilians and soldiers. These organisations also help to protect the lives of civilians by evacuating them if they are in danger and by educating soldiers not to attack them.

What can you do?

Find out more about the work of the Red Cross and Red Crescent Movement on their website. See how you can support them at https://www.icrc.org/en/support-us.

Life in a WARZONE

According to the international laws of war, only soldiers can legally be attacked during a civil war or any other type of war. It is illegal to attack civilians. However, civilians are inevitably nearly always caught up the middle of civil wars. Fighting moves into residential areas and ordinary people are recruited into the army.

Unoccupied areas

Restricting fighting to unoccupied areas is the most effective way to protect civilians during war. This can be complicated for armies, as they have to bring their own supplies, shelters and equipment. However, there are fewer places for enemies to hide and they do not have to worry about civilians becoming caught in the crossfire.

Towns and cities

Fighting in civil wars often moves into towns and cities. This is more convenient for the soldiers as they have easier access to resources and supplies. Urban areas are easier to defend, as there are many places for soldiers to hide and strategically attack the enemy. However, this also makes life extremely dangerous for the civilian residents. People are accidentally injured in crossfire between the two sides. Snipers on both sides shoot at anyone, civilian or soldier, who ventures into the streets.

A fruit seller in Lebanon runs from a sniper attack in 2013. Fighting from the Syrian civil war crossed over into Lebanon, putting many people at risk.

Bombs

One of the greatest dangers of fighting in towns and cities is the use of destructive and powerful bombs. When armies drop bombs from planes or set off mines, they can't always control what gets destroyed. Homes and hospitals are blown up by mistake, or even deliberately, and many civilians lose their lives.

New recruits

During a civil war, ordinary people are often encouraged to join the army. Most soldiers are men, but in some cases, women and even children are accepted into the army. Some people join willingly and happily fight for what they believe in. Others are forced to fight and trained to obey orders, without thinking of the consequences. They may even be ordered to torture civilians or carry out massacres.

Child soldiers

In some civil wars, armies will recruit children from poor backgrounds to fight on their side, as child soldiers can be valuable weapons. It is often much easier to manipulate children and they will follow orders easily. They may not understand the danger of weapons, and will do risky things that adults will not. Child soldiers are often left with psychological damage, as they are scarred by their experience of war, as well as neglect and abuse from other soldiers.

This photo of a twelve-year-old child soldier was taken in Sudan in 1999. He was fighting in the army of the Sudanese People's Liberation Movement (SPLM) in the Sudanese civil war (1983-2005). The SPLM were a guerrilla group who opposed the Sudanese government.

Food

Countries in the middle of war often experience food shortages. It is much harder for a country to grow enough food to support itself during a war. People are taken away from agricultural jobs to serve in the army. Agricultural areas turn into battlefields, where nothing can be grown.

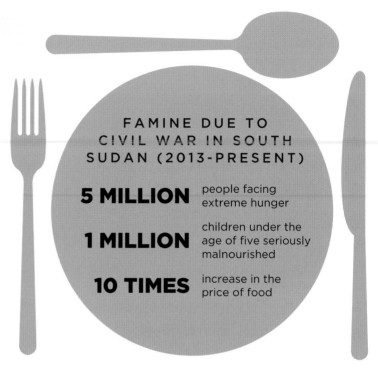

FAMINE DUE TO CIVIL WAR IN SOUTH SUDAN (2013-PRESENT)

5 MILLION people facing extreme hunger

1 MILLION children under the age of five seriously malnourished

10 TIMES increase in the price of food

International trade

When a country is at war, it is harder for it to trade with other countries. It may be too dangerous for planes or boats to enter the country. Some countries may choose to sanction (stop trading with) a country if they don't politically agree with the war, so as to stop providing funds for the rulers. When international trade stops, it can be hard for a country to get important supplies, such as medicine and fuel for its citizens.

Basic services

Civilians living in a warzone often lose access to basic services, such as hospitals, schools and clean water. These services are left understaffed if their employees flee or are injured or killed. These buildings can also be destroyed accidentally during airstrikes or deliberately targeted as a way of punishing the enemy.

CASE STUDY

Diseases in Syria

Thanks to vaccinations, diseases such as measles, tuberculosis, whooping cough and polio are relatively rare in most countries today. However, these diseases are starting to affect children in Syrian refugee camps, as they do not have access to healthcare and vaccinations to protect them. The poor sanitation and living conditions in the camps makes it even easier for children to get sick.

Under siege

The challenges of living in a warzone are made worse when people are forced to live under siege. During a siege, the military blocks people from entering or leaving a settlement. This can be for the civilians' own safety, or as a way of discouraging the enemy from attacking. Food, medicine and fuel are hard to come by during a siege. People have limited access to healthcare, education and sanitation.

This child is playing in the Syrian city of Homs during the period when it was under siege (May 2011 to May 2014). Many people in Syria have had to endure sieges during the civil war.

Fleeing from WAR

Before and during a civil war, many civilians are forced to leave their homes due to fighting or the threat of violence. These people are known as refugees.

Becoming a refugee

Most refugees do not have time to prepare to leave. They can only take what they can carry. They have to leave behind their homes, most of their possessions and many valuable and sentimental items.

Refugee camps

Refugee camps are set up in countries experiencing civil war or other conflicts. These are safe places where refugees can live while the conflict is resolved. Sometimes, refugee camps are protected by peacekeeping troops. Refugee camps can also be set up in nearby countries for extra security.

Somali refugees collect water in the Dadaab refugee camp in Kenya. Dadaab is the largest refugee camp in the world, housing over 250,000 refugees from Somalia, South Sudan, Eritrea and other African countries.

Housing

Refugee camps have temporary housing for refugees to stay in. They often have basic tents or shelters, with little protection against the hot sun, rain or the cold. As refugees arrive in the camps without many possessions, it can be hard for them to protect themselves against the elements with no clothes or blankets for warmth.

Long-term problems

Refugee camps are supposed to be temporary, so they do not always have good sanitation or access to schools and healthcare. This creates problems if a conflict goes on for a long time. Poor sanitation and lack of healthcare lead to disease (see page 21). Children living in refugee camps miss out on years of education.

This woman and her family live in a tent in a refugee camp on the Syrian/Turkish border. She is preparing food on a stove she made herself.

Going home

Many refugees want to return to their home country. They wait for peace so that they can go back and rebuild their lives. However, there are also occasions when refugees cannot return home.

A new country

Refugees move on to other countries for many reasons. For some people, it is too dangerous for them to return home if their political enemies have won the war. If a war goes on for a long time, people may choose to move to other countries so that their children can get an education and they can carry on working. Other people who have lost everything in the war might want to start again in a place without painful memories.

Applying for asylum

Refugees who want to move to another country have to apply for asylum. This gives them the right to remain in another country for their own protection. Many countries take in refugees that have completed the application process. However, the application process can be long, difficult and expensive, which makes it hard for some refugees to find safety.

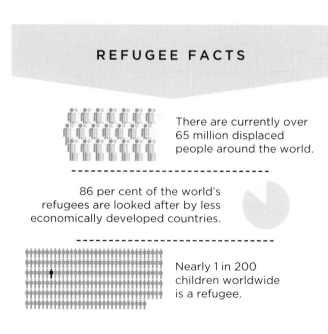

REFUGEE FACTS

There are currently over 65 million displaced people around the world.

86 per cent of the world's refugees are looked after by less economically developed countries.

Nearly 1 in 200 children worldwide is a refugee.

Illegal immigration

Refugees can often feel desperate while their application for asylum is being considered. The process moves slowly and some countries do not accept many asylum seekers. In some cases, refugees decide to illegally enter a country, rather than waiting for the legal right to enter. They cross borders on foot or pay people traffickers to help them enter by boat.

CASE STUDY

European refugee crisis

Since 2015, many more refugees from the Middle East and Africa have been arriving in Europe by boat or on foot. Many of them are fleeing civil wars, such as the conflict in Syria. Others from Iraq and Afghanistan are looking for a new life after years of conflict. A number of economic migrants have also started crossing into Europe, looking for better job prospects. As these people are entering illegally, their transport is unregulated and very dangerous. Many refugees and migrants have drowned trying to reach Europe on crowded, unsafe boats.

These refugees are travelling from Hungary to Germany on foot. Countries such as Hungary have closed their borders to the refugees, while Germany has given asylum to over 140,000 people.

What can you do? Find out about projects welcoming refugees in your local area. See if you can attend an event where you can meet and get to know refugees, or donate items that they might need, such as clothing, toiletries and food.

Human rights are rights that apply to everyone in the world, regardless of where they live or what they do. In some places, people are not given the human rights that are legally theirs. Being a civilian victim of a civil war or genocide are two ways in which people's humans rights can be abused.

Rights in history

Throughout history, people have made rules about rights, such as the right to own land or the right to an education. In the past, these rules did not apply to everyone and mainly benefited rich, powerful men. Women, members of minority groups and poor people did not enjoy the same rights as others.

The United Nations

A vast number of human rights abuses took place during the Second World War. Civilians were killed, tortured and forced to leave their home countries. When the war ended in 1945, an international organisation called the United Nations (UN) was set up to protect human rights. Representatives from different countries came together to encourage peace and cooperation around the world.

Flags of some of the countries that make up the UN fly outside its headquarters in New York, USA.

The Universal Declaration of Human Rights

The newly formed United Nations started work on the Universal Declaration of Human Rights – a legal document that states the human rights that apply to everyone on Earth. They needed to produce this legal document so that they could prosecute people who did not follow what it said. The declaration was first signed on 10 December 1948; today, many countries have signed the declaration and promised to follow its rules.

SOME UNIVERSAL HUMAN RIGHTS

The right to life, liberty and security

The right not to be enslaved

The right to own property

The right to an education

The right to freedom of movement

The right not to be subjected to torture or cruel treatment

The right to have and change your religion

The right to freedom of thought and expression

The right to marry and to have a family

The right to work

The right to leave any country and return to your own country

The right not to be arrested, imprisoned or exiled for no reason

Human rights and war

In times of war, it can be difficult to establish human rights, especially the human rights of soldiers. Soldiers have (usually) willingly agreed to take part in war. For this reason, it isn't illegal for a soldier to kill another soldier and take away their right to life. This isn't considered to be murder, as murder is illegally killing someone.

The Geneva Conventions

If a soldier is taken captive or injured in battle, different rights apply to him or her. At this point, the soldier is protected by the Geneva Conventions – a set of international laws that protect the human rights of people who are in warzones, but who are not fighting.

The Geneva Conventions protect captive and wounded soldiers who can no longer fight, as well as doctors, aid workers and civilians. The Geneva Conventions were created in 1864, but revised after the Second World War, in response to the poor treatment of soldiers and civilians during the war.

Wounded soldiers

According to the Geneva Conventions, wounded soldiers must not be attacked. They must be allowed to travel to hospital and receive treatment. Uninjured soldiers can evacuate fellow troops without the risk of being fired at.

These US soldiers are practising a medical evacuation during a training exercise. They have lit a flare to show that they are dealing with an injured soldier.

Prisoners of war

Soldiers who are captured by the enemy also have rights according to the Geneva Conventions. They cannot be tortured or treated cruelly. They must be given food, shelter and access to medical treatment. At the end of the war, they must be returned to their home countries, unless they are on trial.

Civilians

According to international law, civilians should not have their human rights violated by war. Their right to life and their right not to be treated cruelly do not change just because they live in a warzone. However, many human rights abuses take place against civilians during and after wars.

Crimes against humanity

Crimes against civilians in times of war are known as crimes against humanity. Crimes against humanity go against the Geneva Conventions and universal human rights laws.

Kidnappings

Massacres

Genocide

CRIMES AGAINST HUMANITY

Torture

Slavery

Persecution

Forcing civilians to work as soldiers

GENOCIDE

Genocide is the attempt to destroy an ethnic, religious, national or racial group. Usually, this is achieved through killing large numbers of people. Injuring or harming people through rape is also considered genocide.

The word 'genocide' was coined in 1943 in a book detailing the Nazi's planned mass murder of certain groups of people during the Second World War. It comes from the Greek word 'genos' (race, people) and the Latin word 'cide' (to kill).

Recent genocides

There have been a number of events during the twentieth and twenty-first centuries that have been officially confirmed as genocides. Some were carried out during international wars, such as the Second World War, while others took place during civil wars, such as the conflict in Yugoslavia. Some genocides have happened during the rule of strict, cruel groups, such as the Khmer Rouge in Cambodia.

TWENTIETH-CENTURY GENOCIDES

Armenia	Cambodia	Yugoslavia	Holocaust
• Year: 1915–1916	• Year: 1975–1979	• Year: 1991–1995	• Year: 1938–1945
• Targeted group: Armenians	• Targeted group: enemies of the Khmer Rouge	• Targeted group: Croats, Bosniaks	• Targeted group: Jewish people, gay people, disabled people, Roma people
• Carried out by: the Ottoman Empire (in present-day Turkey)	• Carried out by: the Khmer Rouge government	• Carried out by: Serbian forces	• Carried out by: Nazi Germany
• Death toll: 1.5 million	• Death toll: 1.7 to 2 million	• Death toll: 8,000 in Srebrenica massacre (see page 17), plus thousands of other victims throughout the war	• Death toll: Jewish people – 6 million / gay people – as high as 60 per cent of the 5,000–15,000 sent to concentration camps / disabled people – 170,000 / Roma people – 200,000

CASE STUDY

Rwandan genocide

The tension between the two ethnic groups in Rwanda – the Hutus (majority) and the Tutsis (minority) – dates back to German and Belgian colonial rule. During the Rwandan civil war (1990–1993), the Hutus spread hateful propaganda about the Tutsis. This created fear among the Hutu population that the Tutsis wanted to kill them and take over the country. Peace deals were in progress in 1994, when the president of Rwanda was killed when his plane was shot down. The Hutu government ordered the military to immediately begin the genocide of the Tutsi people. Many ordinary people also took part, motivated by the propaganda they had seen. In 100 days, over 800,000 people were killed. The victims were mainly Tutsis, but many moderate Hutu leaders were also killed.

Before a genocide

Genocides don't happen overnight. In the period before a genocide, people in power create fear and hatred of a minority group and make them seem less than human. Once ordinary people fear those in the minority and have stopped considering them as their equals, it's much easier for the people in charge to convince others to commit genocide.

The Kigali Genocide Memorial Centre exhibits photos of some of the children who were killed during the Rwandan genocide. The centre honours those who lost their lives and has exhibitions explaining how the genocide came to happen and its aftermath.

Ten stages of genocide

Dr Gregory Stanton, the president of Genocide Watch (an organisation that aims to end genocide), published a report called 'Ten stages of genocide' in 2013.

The ten stages of genocide and how to fight back

Stage	1	2	3	4	5
Signs	People are classified by ethnicity, religion or race. People think about different groups as 'us and them'.	People in a minority group are forced to wear hateful symbols that mark them as different.	The minority group loses its civil rights or right to citizenship.	Propaganda is published that describes the minority group as 'not human'.	Leaders begin planning how the genocide will take place. They sometimes train militia groups (troops that do not belong to a country's army), so that the leaders can deny later that they were involved.
What can be done?	Create groups of mixed people that encourage cooperation and tolerance. Find common ground with people who are different to you.	Ban hateful symbols, such as the yellow Jewish star. Refuse to make people wear hateful symbols.	Sue the government or any group who abuses or removes anyone's civil rights.	Condemn the use of hate speech and propaganda. Punish hate crimes. Impose sanctions on leaders who allow hate speech or encourage it.	Ban people from joining militia groups. Ban the sale of weapons to these groups.

2 – In Nazi Germany, Jewish people were forced to wear a yellow star on their clothes.

4 – In Rwanda, Tutsis were referred to as 'cockroaches' in the media. In the UK, the newspaper columnist Katie Hopkins also used the word 'cockroaches' to describe migrants in 2015.

5 – In 2003, the Sudanese government gave weapons and resources to the Janjaweed militia. The militia carried out genocide on the government's behalf, but the government later denied any connection to the Janjaweed.

In the report, it describes the ten steps that often lead to genocide. According to Dr Stanton, the steps do not always happen in this order, but the earlier stages will always lead to later stages unless people stand up for what is right and fight back.

6	7	8	9	10
Extreme laws that ban marriage or interaction between the minority group and other people are introduced. People who speak out in support of the minority are arrested or killed.	Leaders prepare for genocide by gathering armies and weapons. They convince civilians that they must kill the minority, or the minority will kill them first.	Members of the minority are sent to ghettos and taken to labour camps. They are starved and their property is stolen. People begin to be killed.	The genocide begins and millions of civilians are deliberately murdered.	After the genocide is over, the guilty leaders deny that any crime took place. They hide evidence, block investigations and flee from the country.
Protect those who support minority groups. Encourage the intervention of human rights groups.	Ban the sale of weapons to these countries. Prosecute anyone who is planning to commit genocide. Freeze the foreign wealth of extremist leaders and ban their foreign travel.	Declare a genocide emergency. Encourage other countries to send peacekeeping troops. Send humanitarian aid organised by the UN and charities.	Protect safe areas and escape routes for refugees. Encourage other countries to send peacekeeping troops.	Launch international investigations and trials for those involved. Prosecute those found guilty and bring them to justice.

8 – The Nazis sent Jewish people to labour and concentration camps, where they were worked to death or killed on arrival.

10 – Pol Pot, the leader of the Khmer Rouge government in Cambodia, was sentenced to house arrest in 1997, but never taken to court or sentenced for the genocide carried out on his orders.

What can you do?

Read and take the pledge against genocide on the Genocide Watch website –http://genocidewatch.net/get-involved-2/pledge-against-genocide/. Spread the word about the pledge to others.

Cultural genocide

Sometimes, people try to wipe out minority groups in ways other than killing them. They destroy their culture or stop people in the group from having children. In this way, the group gets smaller over time. This is sometimes known as cultural genocide.

Sterilisation

The Nazis sterilised over 400,000 people, including many mixed-race people. They wanted to create a society in which Aryan (blonde, blue-eyed) people were in control, so different racial groups were not allowed to marry each other and reproduce.

Children and culture

A common way of destroying minority cultures is to force children from the group to leave their community and stop following their traditional customs. The children are made to attend boarding schools, far away from their families. They are not allowed to speak their own languages or learn about their culture. Eventually, the culture dies out because there are no younger generations to continue and pass on their traditions.

BOARDING SCHOOLS

The US government forced Native American Indian children to attend boarding schools in the late nineteenth and early twentieth centuries.

In Canada, indigenous children were made to attend boarding schools up until 1996.

Stolen generations

Up until the 1970s, the Australian government forcibly separated thousands of Australian Aboriginal and Torres Strait Islander children from their families. The government claimed that the children would have better lives in boarding schools, but many children suffered serious abuse there. When the children finished school, they were sent away from home again to work at poorly paid jobs. The Australian government has since apologised and organised a remembrance day to commemorate those who suffered. However, there are still far more Aboriginal children removed from their parents' care and taken into foster care than any other group in Australia.

Aboriginal people only make up

3 PER CENT
of the population in Australia.

ONE THIRD
of children removed from their families are Aboriginal.

These protesters in Brisbane in 2014 are carrying a banner reading, 'Sorry means you don't do it again'. This refers to the high number of Aboriginal children who are still being removed from their parents today.

Speaking up

One way of preventing future genocides is to resist all forms of discrimination. We should speak up if we see people being treated differently because of their ethnicity, race, nationality, gender or sexuality. It is also important to educate people about minority groups, so that they don't get incorrect information from propaganda.

Examining the facts

Today, people can publish anything online, regardless of whether or not it is true. It's important to make sure we get our facts from reliable sources that support their claims with evidence. Nearly all newspapers and websites have a slanted political opinion that influences how they report events. They use emotional language and may use fake news stories to convince their readers to share their ideas. This can be dangerous if the newspaper's views are hateful, as many people may read the so-called news source and go on to develop similar opinions.

The newspaper headlines in the UK on the day before the EU referendum reflected each publication's political opinion.

These people in Berlin, Germany, have organised a protest to criticise new laws in Russia that ban people from saying that LGBT relationships are normal.

Thinking bigger

On a bigger scale, how can hate groups and political parties who spread harmful messages about minority groups be stopped? We can stop money going to countries that abuse human rights by not visiting or buying products from them. Ignore people who deny past genocides or human rights abuses.

What can you do?

Interact with people who are different to you. Find out about their lives and get to know them. The more that we do this, the easier it is to see that we all have things in common.

The end of a civil war is a time of both celebration and sadness. Survivors have to begin the long process of rebuilding their lives and their communities. They must deal with the practical problems that are consequences of war, while having to cope with grief, shock and trauma.

Men and women

Civil wars and genocide affect the population structure of a country. Men are more likely to serve in the military than women, and therefore are more likely to be killed or injured. This means that countries often have more women than men after a war.

Supporting a family

The loss of large numbers of men is a problem in countries where men are expected to work to support their families. If a large proportion of these men die, many families are left with no breadwinner. In this situation, widowed women have to go to work instead. However, many of these women did not receive a good education. They are unprepared for higher-skilled jobs that allow them to earn enough money to support themselves well in the long term.

Professional workers

Countries are often left without professional workers, such as doctors and lawyers, after civil wars. This is because people with higher levels of education and more access to money find it easier to leave and support themselves elsewhere. These skilled people establish themselves abroad, leaving their home countries with a 'brain drain', or lack of skilled professionals, when peace is declared.

Food and famine

After a war, it can be hard for a country to produce enough food to support its citizens. There are fewer people to grow food and process it in factories. People stop planting crops during war, so there may not even be any food to harvest. It is hard to plant new crops when fighting has destroyed agricultural areas. Food shortages can quickly lead to famine, so people should return to farming as soon as possible.

This boy is selling onions in a refugee camp in South Sudan. South Sudan is now facing a famine after many years of drought and conflict, during which people were unable to plant crops.

What can you do?

Support charities, such as Oxfam, who help people to find sustainable ways of making a living after civil wars. In Rwanda, Oxfam is training widows to run businesses supplying pineapples to larger companies, so that they can support their families well.

New leaders

At the end of a civil war, a country may be given the option to choose a new government to replace previous leaders who were defeated in the war. It can be hard for a country to choose and trust new leaders, especially when disagreement could lead to another war.

Other countries sometimes intervene in this process and help to put their preferred party into power. This can be done with good intentions, for example, helping to run democratic elections after the end of a dictatorship. However, it can also be an excuse for foreign countries to manipulate events for their own benefit, such as helping to elect a leader who offers them good trade deals.

Improving society

After a war, it's important to find solutions to problems such as unemployment and corruption. These problems create an unequal society, which makes people feel unhappy and frustrated. These feelings lead to disagreements, and even war. Improving people's quality of life makes it less likely that a conflict will happen again in the future. Other countries and organisations such as the UN can provide support during this process.

Rebuilding

As well as rebuilding politics and communities, a country has to rebuild its cities and towns after war. On many occasions, buildings and roads are damaged by bombs or bullets. When people flee their hometowns, houses and other buildings are left abandoned and become run down. These structures need to be repaired so that returning people have places to live and work.

The city of Sarajevo, in Bosnia and Herzegovina, was left ruined after a four-year-long siege during the war in the former Yugoslavia. The city has now been totally rebuilt.

Hidden weapons

Fighting can leave dangerous remains behind. Armies sometimes bury weapons such as grenades and land mines in the ground. If soldiers do not keep accurate records of the location of these weapons, it can be hard to clear them away after the war has ended. These weapons stay active and can cause great harm to civilians if they are accidentally set off later.

CASE STUDY

Land mines in Cambodia

During the Khmer Rouge's rule of Cambodia (1975–1979) and time as a rebel group (1975–1997), different groups placed large numbers of land mines across rural areas of the country to defend towns and villages. People quickly forgot where the mines were placed, and many still remain in remote areas. Even today, many people in rural areas are killed or injured by land mines while farming or foraging for food. Travel and agriculture is challenging, as large areas of land are too dangerous to enter. It is a long and difficult process to find and remove the land mines, but new robotic technology and trained dogs are helping to speed up the process.

Deaths caused
by land mines in
Cambodia since 1979

R.I.P.

64,000

Number of
amputees today

OVER 25,000

LAND
MINE
FACTS

Cost to make
a land mine

$

US$3

Cost to remove
a land mine

$

OVER US$1,000

It can be hard for countries to move on after war, especially in the case of a civil war, where communities may have been turned against each other. Holding people accountable for war crimes and acknowledging what happened during the war are two important steps forward.

War trials

Today, people who carry out war crimes or crimes against humanity (see page 29) can be prosecuted for their crimes. These trials are often held in international criminal courts. Judges and lawyers from around the world work together on these cases, which can take place in any country.

The Nuremberg trials

The laws used to prosecute war criminals today date back to the events of the Nuremberg trials, which were held to prosecute Nazi war criminals after the Second World War.

Important members of the Nazi Party stood trial for crimes against humanity, such as genocide, and war crimes, such as murdering and abusing prisoners of war and civilians.

CASE STUDY

The Eichmann trial

Adolf Eichmann was a high-ranking member of the Nazi Party. After the Second World War, he was tried for his role in carrying out genocide and coordinating the deaths of millions of Jewish people in the Holocaust. Although his crimes were carried out in Europe, it was decided that Eichmann could be tried in Israel. Eichmann used the defence that he had just been following orders, but he was found guilty of war crimes, crimes against Jewish people and crimes against humanity. He was executed by hanging in 1962.

Placing the blame

During the Nuremberg trials, lawyers needed to establish who was responsible for crimes such as genocide. Although many individual soldiers carried out the genocide, they were acting on orders from their leaders. In the trials, it was decided that 'following orders' was not a suitable defence, although it could be taken into account when deciding on a sentence. The lawyers also ruled that high-ranking leaders who planned large-scale crimes could be held responsible for those who carried out their orders.

On trial

These rulings are still used today. For example, the leaders who organised genocide during the civil war in what was Yugoslavia have been prosecuted for crimes against humanity, although they did not carry out the massacres themselves. Radovan Karadžić, the former leader of the Bosnian Serbs, was found guilty of genocide and nine other war crimes in 2016. He was sentenced to 40 years in prison.

Bosnian Muslim women who lost family members in the Srebrenica massacre watch the trial of Radovan Karadžić.

Remember or forget?

After neighbours have fought against each other in a civil war, it seems hard to imagine how they would be able to go back to living alongside each other in peace. Some people wonder whether it's better to try to forget the events of war, or to remember and acknowledge what happened.

Public remembrance

Many people agree that it is important to publically remember wars and human rights abuses. These events are less likely to happen again if people remember the horror of them. Building public memorials and holding days of remembrance are two ways of commemorating past events and paying respect to those who lost their lives.

On 24 April, people gather at the Armenian Genocide memorial complex to observe Armenian Genocide Remembrance Day.

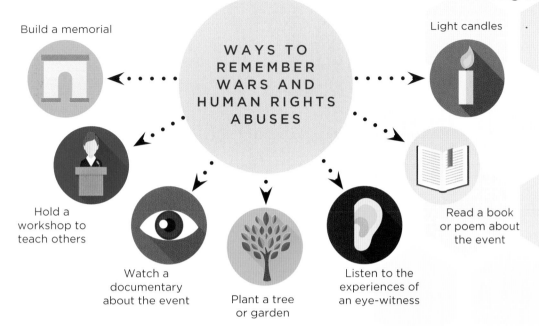

Build a memorial

Light candles

WAYS TO REMEMBER WARS AND HUMAN RIGHTS ABUSES

Hold a workshop to teach others

Watch a documentary about the event

Plant a tree or garden

Listen to the experiences of an eye-witness

Read a book or poem about the event

Forgiveness

Once people have been held accountable for any crimes and received their sentence, many people find it helps them to forgive their enemies and move on. There are losses on both sides in every war and everyone suffers. Holding a grudge or looking for revenge is only going to make matters worse. In the worst case, it could even lead to another civil war.

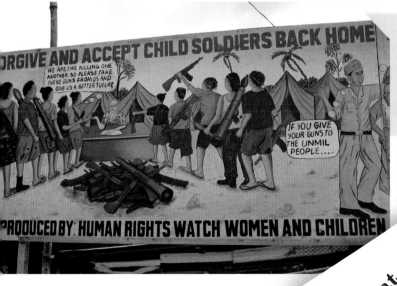

This poster at a refugee camp in Liberia encourages people to accept child soldiers back home if they give up their weapons and stop fighting.

What can you do?

Observe Holocaust Memorial Day on 27 January. This day also commemorates people who lost their lives and lost loved ones in subsequent genocides, such as in Rwanda. Find out about events on this day at http://hmd.org.uk/page/what-you-can-do.

GLOSSARY

airstrike – an attack by military planes that drop bombs

asylum seeker – someone who is applying for the right to live in another country because it is too dangerous for them to live in their home country

capitalism – a political and economic system in which individuals make money by controlling the production of goods

ceasefire – an agreement between two armies to stop fighting

censor – to remove information in books, films or the media so that people can't see it or learn about it

civilian – someone who is not a member of the military

colonise – to take control of and rule over another country

communism – a political system in which the government controls the production of goods and in theory provides people with everything that they need to live

corruption – when people in power behave in a dishonest or immoral way

coup – when a group of people take control of a country using force

crossfire – when bullets come at you from different directions

dictatorship – a country ruled by a dictator, who has complete control and usually has not been legally elected

displaced – describes a person who has been forced to leave their home

extremist – describes very strong views or behaviour that most people do not agree with

famine – a period when people in an area suffer and die because they do not have enough food

genocide – the attempt to destroy an ethnic, religious, national or racial group

massacre – the killing of a lot of people

militia – a group of trained soldiers who are not part of a country's army

neglect – to not give enough care or attention to someone

propaganda – false information or ideas that are shared to persuade people to agree with a particular point of view

prosecute – to accuse someone of a crime in court

proxy war – a war in which two or more opposing sides avoid direct war with each other and instead, fight each other indirectly by supporting opposing sides in another war

sanitation – a system to remove dirt and waste

siege – a period when an army stops people and supplies from leaving or entering a city

Soviet Union – a huge state made up of communist republics, which lasted from 1917 to 1991. Today, the former Soviet Union has been divided up into countries such as Russia, Lithuania, Ukraine and Uzbekistan.

sterilise – to perform an operation on someone so that they can't have children

terrorism – using violence to create fear for political reasons

torture – to cause someone pain to force them to tell you something

vaccinate – to give someone something to stop them from getting a disease

violate – to not obey a rule or a law

FURTHER INFORMATION

Books

Did Anything Good Come Out Of The Cold War/World War Two?
Paul Mason/Emma Marriott (Franklin Watts, 2015)

Why Do We Fight?: Conflict, War and Peace
Niki Walker (Franklin Watts, 2014)

Uprisings in the Middle East (Behind the News)
Philip Steele (Wayland, 2014)

Websites

Find out more about civil war and genocide on these websites:

http://www.bbc.co.uk/newsround/16979186
Background information on the civil war in Syria

http://genocidewatch.net
Resources about the history of genocide and the ten stages of genocide

https://www.dkfindout.com/uk/history/world-war-ii/holocaust/
Facts and further information about the Holocaust

INDEX

OUR WORLD IN CRISIS

9781445163710 9781445163734 9781445163772 9781445163758 9781445163819 9781445163796

Civil War and Genocide
978 1 4451 6371 0

Modern civil wars
War begins
Warfare
Life in a warzone
Fleeing from war
Human rights
Genocide
After a war
Moving on

Global Pollution
978 1 4451 6373 4

What is pollution?
The past
Air pollution
Soil pollution
Water pollution
Our changing climate
People and pollution
The future

Health and Disease
978 1 4451 6377 2

What are health and
　disease?
A healthy lifestyle
A healthy environment
Diseases
Fighting diseases
How diseases spread
Healthcare industries
Improving world health
The future

Immigration
978 1 4451 6375 8

What is immigration?
The past
The facts
Forced to flee
A better life
The impact of immigration
Arguing about
　immigration
The future

Poverty
978 1 4451 6381 9

What is poverty?
Why are people poor?
Who is poor?
Rights for life
Global goals
Action against
　poverty

Terrorism
978 1 4451 6379 6

What is terrorism?
History of terrorism
Religious terrorism
Political terrorism
Facts about terrorism
Fighting terrorism
Does terrorism work?
Responses to terrorism

W
FRANKLIN WATTS
LONDON•SYDNEY